NORTHWEST MONTANA FIRE LOOKOUTS

A HIKING GUIDE

VOLUME TWO

BY

STEVE RAINS

PHOTOGRAPHY

BY

LYNNE RAINS

STEVE RAINS

NORTHWEST MONTANA FIRE LOOKOUTS

VOLUME TWO

A HIKING GUIDE

STEVE RAINS

COPYRIGHT 2017 STEVE RAINS
ISBN: 978-0-9889480-2-0
LIBRARY OF CONGRESS CONTROL NUMBER: 2013931769
FIRST EDITION

PROUDLY MADE IN MONTANA
PROUDLY PRINTED IN THE USA

ALL RIGHTS RESERVED

PUBLISHED AND DISTRIBUTED BY:

DISCOVER MONTANA GUIDEBOOKS LLC
PO BOX 8178
KALISPELL, MONTANA 59904
LIKE US ON FACEBOOK @ DISCOVER MONTANA GUIDEBOOKS
COVER DESIGN BY TRICIA BURRY   INSPIRE COMMUNICATIONS
FRONT COVER: KEELER MOUNTAIN
BACK COVER: PRISCILLA PEAK

TABLE OF CONTENTS

LEGAL NOTICE

Northwest Montana Fire Lookouts Volume Two is not a wilderness survival guide. There is inherent risk every time one drives and hikes in remote areas. The author, photographer, and publisher of this book are not responsible if you or anyone in your party is injured while hiking or driving to one of these hikes and/or locations.

Participation in these activities may result in injury or illness including, but not limited to, bodily injury, disease, strains, fractures, partial or total paralysis, disabilities or death.

These risks and dangers may be caused by negligence of the participants, negligence of others, accidents, forces of nature, or other foreseeable or unforeseeable causes such as poor decision-making, including misjudging terrain, trail, lookout ladders/stairs, falling, animal attack, weather, etc.

ADDITIONAL HIKING GUIDES AVAILABLE TO PURCHASE!

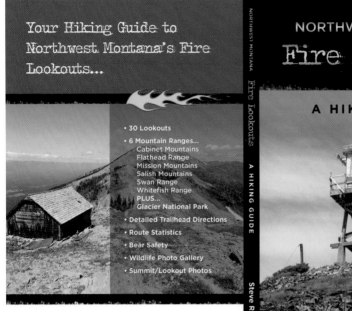

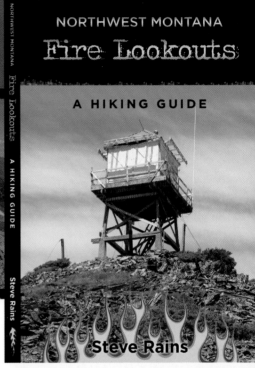

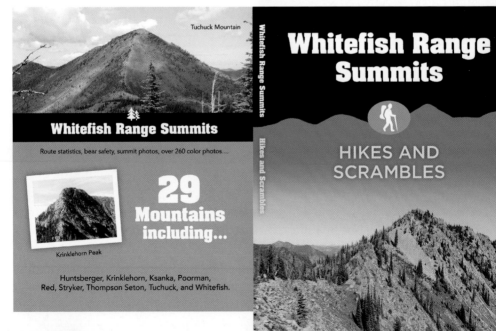

FOR DAVE AND ROBERTA

PSALM 90:2

BEFORE THE MOUNTAINS WERE BROUGHT FORTH, OR EVER THOU HADST FORMED THE EARTH AND THE WORLD, EVEN FROM EVERLASTING TO EVERLASTING, THOU ART GOD.

ACKNOWLEDGEMENTS

I am forever grateful to my intrepid hiking partner, photographer, and best friend. All who happen to be my wife, Lynne! Without her, these books would not be possible! I have been blessed with someone who loves to get out there just as much, if not more so, than myself.

SUMMIT OF PRISCILLA PEAK

MISSION STATEMENT

It is our goal to produce simple, easy-to-read, easy-to-use guide books showcasing the natural beauty and wonder that exists in ALL of Northwest Montana's forests and mountain ranges using compelling photography.

ABOUT THIS BOOK

Thanks for picking up this book! If you've purchased one of our other books you know that our books are primarily photo driven. I firmly believe in the old saying, "that a picture is worth a thousand words." Since I believe that to be true, then seeing it for yourself must be worth "a million words". So, if at all possible, I encourage you to get out there and discover Montana for yourself.

If you've purchased the first volume of Northwest Montana Fire Lookouts, you will also notice that the format of this second volume is somewhat different. There are no separate "mountain range" introduction pages, just the location of the lookout in it's particular range on the beginning page of each lookout.

There are no maps in this book. My books are designed to be used in conjunction with national forest and specific ranger district maps which are easily found throughout northwest Montana. Any map included in a book of this size simply would not have enough detail of the specific area that is being hiked or of the surrounding area, particularly of the conflagration of the many FS Roads it sometimes takes to get to where you want to be. BUY MAPS AND STUDY THEM!

Having said that, several of these lookouts have more than one way to the top. We only feature the way that we did it. Buying maps certainly increases the options for getting to the summits of these mountains.

Most of these featured routes are roads. The beauty of hiking up a road is the ability to customize the hike to your fitness level. Many of these can be started earlier or later on the road than where we did, thus making the hike more difficult, or easier, it is up to you!

Always be prepared for the constant change of mountain weather. We have personally stood on all of these summits and have tried to be as accurate as possible in our descriptions.

In Montana, the Kaniksu National Forest is administered by the Kootenai National Forest.

VITAL STATISTICS

This page explains the statistical data presented on each lookout's first page.

ELEVATION: Simply put, the highest point on the mountain, in feet, above sea level.

ELEVATION GAIN: The amount of height, in feet, gained from the vehicle to the lookout/summit. This number is determined by a combination of a Garmin Etrex Vista HCX GPS unit and topographic maps.

ROUTE DESCRIPTION: Describes how the lookout/summit was achieved, whether by a Forest Service Road, trail, or bushwhack, or a combination of any of the three.

DIFFICULTY: The most subjective category on this list. These descriptions, easy, moderate, and difficult apply to MY fitness level when the hike occurred. These descriptions would apply to many others, but certainly not everyone, as some are in worse shape and others in better shape. Use common sense in determining your fitness level!

ROUND TRIP MILEAGE: The length, in miles, hiked from vehicle to the lookout/summit, and then back to the vehicle. Mileages were measured with the same accurate Garmin Etrex Vista HCX GPS unit.

SOLITUDE SCORE: Honestly, one of the main reasons many of us escape to the mountains at every opportunity is to "throw off" the trappings of civilization. One of my goals is to minimize the prospect of seeing other people. The "Solitude Score" is easily determined. A maximum score of 30 is achieved by not seeing people at any of three points along the trip, the trail head, any point along the trail, and the lookout/summit . Each location is worth 10 points. Seeing people at all three points scores a zero.

AREA/RANGE: The specific mountain range or general area that the lookout is located in.

RESOURCES

Before going out there, especially early in the season, it is always a good idea to check with the corresponding ranger station to determine whether the hike can be completed in a safe manner. Snow levels, when the trail was cleared last, whether gates are open, or if there are any special road projects. These are things that can ruin your day if you're ill prepared.

CSKT (FLATHEAD) RESERVATION

406-675-2700
www.csktribes.org

KOOTENAI NATIONAL FOREST

SUPERVISOR'S OFFICE 406-293-6211

CABINET RANGER DISTRICT 406-827-3533

LIBBY RANGER DISTRICT 406-293-7773

REXFORD RANGER DISTRICT 406-296-2536

THREE RIVERS RANGER DISTRICT 406-295-4693

www.fs.usda.gov/kootenai/

LOLO NATIONAL FOREST

SUPERVISOR'S OFFICE 406-329-3750

NINEMILE RANGER DISTRICT 406-626-5201

PLAINS/THOMPSON FALLS RANGER DISTRICT 406-826-3821

SEELEY LAKE RANGER DISTRICT 406-677-2233

SUPERIOR RANGER DISTRICT 406-822-4233

www.fs.usda.gov/lolo/

BEARS

Hiking in Northwest Montana can be a truly uplifting experience. For me, it's more than just about the awe-inspiring scenery, it's also about what sort of critters can be lurking about while you're getting your outdoor fix. Of course, I'm referring to all sorts of critters, but with a special emphasis on bears.

As stated in our earlier books, we are not bear experts, but do spend a considerable amount of time out there with these fellows, enough time over the years to have had nine close encounters. We try to do everything right, we make lots of noise at regular intervals, particularly around running water, at bends in trails, when it's windy, and sometimes that is still not enough and the bear doesn't hear you. We do carry bear spray and have been fortunate enough to have never had to deploy it in any of these nine situations.

Anyone who says that they can predict an individual bear's behavior is just kidding themselves. Sure, there are behavioral patterns, but bears are like people....they are individuals and have differing temperaments. I'm sure bears "can have a bad day" just like you and I.

So, if you're going to hike in this part of Montana it is important to know the difference between grizzlies and black bears and what to do if you are lucky enough to see a wild bear up close and personal.

SWAN RANGE BLACK BEAR
WITH ATTITUDE!

You should always react to what the bear does, not have the bear react to what you do. Typically, give them enough time to realize that you're a human and they can't run away fast enough. Do your best to know the species!

Color is not a reliable indicator of species. A prime example is the photo above of the blonde/cinnamon phase of a black bear. Both species come in a variety of colors. Grizzlies have a large shoulder hump and the rear is lower than the hump. Typically, a grizzly's claws are visible, like the one in the photo below, while a black bear's are not. Black bear ears are typically taller and straighter while a grizzly ear is shorter and more rounded. However, all characteristics are relative, depending on the bears age and size.

Prevailing theory, if attacked, is fight a black bear because it will not stop until it kills and eats you. A grizzly attack, typically, will end when it no longer perceives you as a threat to it or it's cubs, so cover vital organs and play dead. CARRY BEAR SPRAY AND KNOW HOW TO USE IT!!!!

SPECIAL CONSIDERATIONS

When approaching any lookout, particularly the derelicts, it is always important to be mindful of any old boards or debris laying about the general area. Many of these locations will have old rusty nails sticking up out of boards with broken glass strewn about. No one wants to step on a rusty nail, much less miles from your vehicle, unless you like lots of blood and tetanus shots.

We also mentioned in the first volume, certain roads in particular that might make some people squeamish. There are a number in this volume that should be mentioned as well. If you are accomplished at driving UP forest service roads in Montana, then this is probably not an issue, but if never having done it or at least on a semi-regular basis, then the following roads, at least in part of their length, left something in the recesses of our mind that we felt worth mentioning:

BALDY-BUCKHORN-ROUGH
BERRAY-ROUGH, DROP OFFS
BIG HOLE-DROP OFFS
EDDY-ROUGH, DROP OFFS
MINTON-ROUGH
MORRELL-ROUGH, DROP OFFS
PISTOL CREEK-ROUGH
SONYOK-ROUGH
STARK-DROP OFFS
UP UP-DROP OFFS

Two of the lookouts in the book are on CSKT (Flathead) Reservation land. Please comply in obtaining the appropriate permit to hike on reservation land. It is a "NONRESERVATION RESIDENT CONSERVATION PERMIT". These are available at outdoor retailers in the Flathead Valley for a nominal fee...well worth the money, in my humble opinion, for the astounding beauty you will see from these two locations. You do not need a reservation fishing license, to hike.....these are considerably more expensive than the standard conservation permit.

Something else that deserves mentioning in this section is hiking through a previous season's forest fire burn area. A devastating forest fire can destroy any trail system in it's path, along with many other things. Always wait for the forest service to re-open an area that has been burned. This is for your SAFETY! Once an area has been re-opened, it is important to follow the precautions specifically spelled out in the picture below. There are three lookouts that are featured that have had fires directly impact the immediate area around them or a portion of the trail system used to reach them.

The Thompson River Fire Complex of 2014 impacted a portion of the trail system to Priscilla Peak. The Berray Mountain Fire of 2015, impacted the road and trail system on this mountain. The Copper King Fire of 2016 impacted the area around the Big Hole Lookout. In at least two of these cases, Priscilla Peak and Big Hole, the wildfire came close enough to have the lookouts wrapped in fire retardant material. On Berray Mountain, you can actually see where the fire burned around and past the rocky knoll that the tower sits on. Be safe out there!

🔥 FOR YOUR SAFETY ⚒

Portions of the area you are entering were burned during recent fires. You may encounter hazards in the forest, be aware of the following:
- UNSTABLE DEAD TREES - especially in windy conditions!
- LOOSE ROCKS & LOGS - watch for rolling debris.
- BURNED-OUT STUMP HOLES - ground may be weak and unstable.
- ASH & NEEDLES ON ROAD - can make roads slippery.
- FLASH FLOODING & MUD FLOWS - especially in areas without vegetation.

CONDITIONS IN A BURNED FOREST CHANGE CONSTANTLY

BE ALERT!

TAKE PROPER SAFETY PRECAUTIONS SUCH AS:
- Assess current weather conditions in the forest.
- Let someone know your destination.
- Locate your camp away from burned trees.

Cabinet Ranger District, 2693 Hwy 200
Trout Creek, MT 59874
(406) 827-3533

RENTALS

Twelve of the lookouts featured in this book are available for rental use by the public. The following list is by the corresponding ranger district within the appropriate national forest. An excellent website, www.recreation.gov, allows you to check availability and to make reservations at your desired lookout.

KOOTENAI/KANIKSU NATIONAL FOREST

CABINET

GEM PEAK
MINTON PEAK
SEX PEAK

REXFORD

WEBB MOUNTAIN

THREE RIVERS

MOUNT BALDY-BUCKHORN RIDGE
BIG CREEK BALDY MOUNTAIN
GARVER MOUNTAIN
YAAK MOUNTAIN

LOLO NATIONAL FOREST

PLAINS/THOMPSON FALLS

COUGAR PEAK

SEELEY LAKE

DOUBLE ARROW LOOKOUT

SUPERIOR

THOMPSON PEAK
UP UP MOUNTAIN

BASIC NAVIGATION

Our home base is Kalispell. Many of the featured lookouts in this book are located to the northwest in Lincoln County and also to the southwest in Sanders County. It would be redundant to give the beginning driving directions over and over again. This page attempts to address that by giving those beginning directions to so many of the lookouts one time. More specific directions will begin in one of the several charming small towns that these routes go through en route to the final destination.

EUREKA--From downtown Whitefish drive approximately 51 miles north on US Highway 93.

LIBBY--From Kalispell drive approximately 87.6 miles west on US Highway 2.

PLAINS--From Kalispell drive south on US Hwy 93 for 35.2 miles to MT Hwy 28 at Elmo. Turn right on Hwy 28 and drive for 46.7 miles to MT Hwy 200. Most of this 46 miles (at least until Hot Springs) is truly "Big Sky Country". The scenery through this portion of the Flathead Indian Reservation (aka CSKT), in my humble opinion, is truly stunning.

ST. REGIS--From Plains, turn left on Hwy 200 and drive for 8.3 miles until reaching MT Hwy 135, after passing through Paradise. Turn right on Hwy 135 and drive south for approximately 21.5 miles to St. Regis.

TROY--From Libby, continue driving west on US Highway 2 for an additional, approximately, 20.4 miles.

MOUNT BALDY
KOOTENAI NATIONAL FOREST
PURCELL MOUNTAINS

ELEVATION: 6529' ELEVATION GAIN: 0
ROUTE DESCRIPTION: ROAD OR TRAIL DIFFICULTY: VARIES
ROUND TRIP MILEAGE: VARIES SOLITUDE SCORE: 30

OVERVIEW

This site (aka as Buckhorn Baldy) was developed around 1910 with a 45' pole platform tower. It was replaced in 1927 by a log cabin with an L-6 cupola. The present 30' treated timber tower with it's L-4 cab was built in 1957.

Spectacular views in all directions, particularly northward, of the Northwest Peak Scenic Area, beginning with Rock Candy Mountain.

GETTING THERE

From Troy, drive 10.2 miles west on Hwy 2. Turn right on Yaak River Road (#508). Drive 17.6 miles north on #508 to Meadow Creek Road (#524). Turn left on #524 and drive .64 miles. Turn right on Hell Roaring Creek Road (#745), which at some point becomes FS Road #591. You can drive to the top of the mountain from here for an additional 12 miles. The last 3.5 miles of this road is EXTREMELY ROCKY!! High clearance not needed, but good tires are strongly suggested.

OSBORNE FIRE FINDER

ROUTE INFORMATION

The only lookout in the book that we did not hike to. We rented this, so we ended up driving to the top. Thus, there is no specific mileage or elevation gain mentioned in the statistics. Park anywhere along the road at a pullout and hike up or take Trail #160 up from #508. The trail is located just a little way north of the turn onto #524.

NORTHWEST PEAK SCENIC AREA

VIEW SOUTH OF PURCELLS

VIEW TO NORTHEAST

SUNSET

BERRAY MOUNTAIN
KOOTENAI NATIONAL FOREST
CABINET MOUNTAINS

ELEVATION: 6177' ELEVATION GAIN: 1160'
ROUTE DESCRIPTION: TRAIL DIFFICULTY: EASY
ROUND TRIP MILEAGE: 4.42 SOLITUDE SCORE: 20

OVERVIEW

This site was first developed around 1931 with a log cabin and a 20' observation platform. This was replaced in 1940 with an L-4 cab on a 50' pole tower. The present 30' treated timber tower with an R-6 flat cab was built in 1965.

In my humble opinion, the views from this lookout are some of the best you will ever see. To the east, the peaks of the Cabinet Mountains Wilderness stretch from north to south as far as the eye can see. To the west, the rugged Scotchmans, among others, are impressive. The lookout had a close call during the Berray Mountain Wildfire of 2015.

GETTING THERE

From Plains, turn right on Hwy 200 and drive 66.2 miles to MT Hwy 56. Turn right and drive north for 8.1 miles. Turn right on FS Road #407 (East Fork Bull River Road). Stay left (on #407) at a junction at 1.33 miles. After an approximately additional 2 miles, turn left on FS Road #410. Stay on #410 for 4.32 miles, going over Snake Creek Pass, and down to the intersection with FS Road #2272. Turn left and drive up the mountain for 6.24 miles to the trail head for Trail #1028. These forest service roads are a little sketchy in places.

ZOOM OF BERRAY FROM STAR

ROUTE INFORMATION

From here, it is a relatively short haul to the lookout. Be careful, as the trail winds it's way through much of the destruction of the Berray Mountain Wildfire of 2015. Do not leave the trail for your own safety. There are some ups and downs along the way so the total gain given is an estimate. Be prepared to be blown away by the mind numbing views, particularly of Billiard Table Mountain to the SW, and many others!

NORTH

IBEX PEAK

ELEPHANT PEAK

WEST

BIG CREEK BALDY

KOOTENAI NATIONAL FOREST
PURCELL MOUNTAINS

ELEVATION: 5768' ELEVATION GAIN: 1008'
ROUTE DESCRIPTION: ROAD DIFFICULTY: EASY
ROUND TRIP MILEAGE: 4.84 SOLITUDE SCORE: 30

OVERVIEW

This site was developed in 1928 with the log cabin pictured left. In 1934, a 30' wooden tower with a 7x7 cab was added. In 1966, that was replaced by the current 41' treated timber tower with R-6 flat cab.

Eye-popping views for 360 degrees reward your efforts at the summit of the Cabinet Mountains Wilderness to the south, and the Purcells in the other three directions. Rock Candy Mountain to the NW, Mount Henry to the north, and further to the NE, Robinson Mountain are all visible. Closer, the ski runs of Turner Mountain beckon for wintertime fun.

GETTING THERE

From Libby, turn right on MT Hwy 37. Drive east for 1.2 miles, then turn left on Pipe Creek Road (#567). Continue north on #567 for 18.3 miles. Turn right on FS Road #336. After approximately 1 mile veer to the right on FS Road #309. We drove up #309 for 3.25 miles and parked.

ROUTE INFORMATION

After hiking up #309 for 1.58 miles and gaining 552', turn right. At 1.66 miles we encountered a closed gate. If you're renting the lookout, you'll have the combination and you can drive all the way up. From here, though, the road gets steep and rocky, possibly requiring high clearance and 4 wheel drive to make it all the way. We continued hiking past the closed gate until reaching the lookout, at 2.42 miles one way and gaining 1008'.

TURNER MOUNTAIN

VIEW TO THE NW

EAST

NORTH

BIG HOLE
LOLO NATIONAL FOREST
CABINET MOUNTAINS

ELEVATION: 6922' ELEVATION GAIN: 1405'
ROUTE DESCRIPTION: TRAIL DIFFICULTY: EASY
ROUND TRIP MILEAGE: 5.46 SOLITUDE SCORE: 30

OVERVIEW

This site was first developed in 1930 with the construction of the original log cabin. This lookout survived the Copper King Fire of 2016.

Views to the east-northeast are dominated by Baldy Mountain. Further to the NE, Thompson Peak is visible. Expansive views to the north include lower peaks of both the Cabinet and Salish Mountains. NW, Priscilla Peak and Mount Headley beckon for future hiking adventures.

GETTING THERE

From Plains, drive west on Hwy 200 for approximately 8.2 miles until reaching Weeksville Creek Road (#887). Turn right, driving for 3.3 miles, until reaching FS Road #5587. Turn left on FS Road #5587 and drive up the mountain for 9.6 miles until reaching the trail head for the Big Hole Lookout Trail #368.

SEPTEMBER 2014

ROUTE INFORMATION

Hike up the trail for 2.47 miles, gaining 1170' in elevation. This is a wide, well maintained trail in September 2014. At this junction, take Trail #386 (signed incorrectly?) up to the lookout for an additional .26 miles and 235' of gain. Soak in the lookout vibe for a while and then we strongly suggest summitting Big Hole Peak, located less than a half mile to the west.

WEST

VIEW TO NE

ZOOM OF BALDY MOUNTAIN

VIEW SE

BLUE MOUNTAIN
KOOTENAI NATIONAL FOREST
PURCELL MOUNTAINS

ELEVATION: 6040' ELEVATION GAIN: NEGLIGIBLE
ROUTE DESCRIPTION: ROAD DIFFICULTY: EASY
ROUND TRIP MILEAGE: .5 SOLITUDE SCORE: 30

OVERVIEW

First developed in 1921 with a crow's nest tree lookout, followed in 1928 by a log cabin. In 1935, the present 72' steel tower was constructed, and a new cabin was built in 1940. That cabin was torn down in 2006. There is also an electronic site at the summit.

Clambering almost the entire way to the top gives one outstanding views of the Cabinet Mountains Wilderness to the southwest and the Purcells in every other direction. Unfortunately, when we were there our long range views were compromised by forest fire smoke from Washington state.

GETTING THERE

From Libby, turn right on MT Hwy 37. Drive east for 1.2 miles, then turn left on Pipe Creek Road (#567). Drive north on #567 for 6.9 miles. Turn right on unmarked #755 (5 mailboxes grouped together). Drive up #755 as far as desired, park where possible, and then hike the rest, or continue all the way to the top in your vehicle.

ROUTE INFORMATION

We drove too far up this road, in my opinion, to get any sort of hiking benefits. There is another approach from the east on Trail #12. This would be a much more rewarding approach as far as exercise and an outdoor experience in the Purcell Mountains.

NORTHWEST

SOUTHWEST

CAMELS HUMP
LOLO NATIONAL FOREST
COEUR D'ALENE MOUNTAINS

ELEVATION: 5888' ELEVATION GAIN: 815'
ROUTE DESCRIPTION: ROAD DIFFICULTY: EASY
ROUND TRIP MILEAGE: 6.28 SOLITUDE SCORE: 30

OVERVIEW

This site was first developed in 1935 with a 20' pole tower with an L-4 cab. It was replaced by the present 41' treated timber tower with an R-6 cab in 1960.

Stunning views of Ward Peak and Eagle Peak south in the Bitterroots are visible before even reaching the summit. Stellar views to the north of Penrose Peak and Cherry Peak offer further possibilities for exploration.

GETTING THERE

From St. Regis, drive west on Mullan Gulch Road (Old Hwy 10) for 7.6 miles to FS Road #3800 (Camels Hump Road) and turn right. We drove up the mountain for 4.07 miles to the first large switchback and hiked it from there. There are many other parking options along the road.

ROUTE INFORMATION

We hiked up the road, through two different gates, one after hiking 1.51 miles and the second at 2.2 miles, to the summit for 3.14 miles one way. There are views along the road in various places. Even though the trap door to the tower was locked, getting up the stairs provides superb views.

WARD PEAK TO SW

NORTH

ZOOM OF PENROSE PEAK

ZOOM OF WARD PEAK

COUGAR PEAK
LOLO NATIONAL FOREST
CABINET MOUNTAINS

ELEVATION: 6694' ELEVATION GAIN: 1145'
ROUTE DESCRIPTION: ROAD DIFFICULTY: EASY
ROUND TRIP MILEAGE: 9.24 SOLITUDE SCORE: 30

OVERVIEW

This site was first developed in 1930 with an L-4 cab. It was replaced with the current L-4 cab in 1952.

Sweeping vistas in every direction reward you at the top. South, the Clark Fork Valley and the Coeur D'Alene Mountains, including Sex Peak to Black Peak on the Idaho border. To the west, more of the Cabinets, to the northwest, the higher peaks of the Cabinet Mountains Wilderness, and more Cabinets to the north and east.

GETTING THERE

From Plains, drive west on Hwy 200 for approximately 43.8 miles to Blue Slide Road, west of Thompson Falls, just before the bridge over the Clark Fork River. Turn right and drive for 7.28 miles to FS Road #403 (Cougar Peak Road). Turn right here. We drove up the mountain for 10.54 miles, parking at the "15th switchback", after encountering a gate at 2.65 miles.

ROUTE INFORMATION

We hiked up the road and encountered a closed gate after 2.71 miles. After hiking an additional 1.91 miles you've reached the summit and the eye candy awaiting there. After spending some time at the lookout, hiking over to Graves Peak on Trail #541, is a worthwhile excursion and highly encouraged!

GRAVES PEAK

BLACK PEAK

SEX PEAK

44

VIEW SE

VIEW NW

45

DOUBLE ARROW
LOLO NATIONAL FOREST
MISSION MOUNTAINS

ELEVATION: 4941' ELEVATION GAIN: 689'
ROUTE DESCRIPTION: ROAD DIFFICULTY: EASY
ROUND TRIP MILEAGE: 3.68 SOLITUDE SCORE: 20

OVERVIEW

This 20' pole tower with it's L-4 cab, staffed into the mid-1980's, was constructed in 1933.

Views from this lookout are surprisingly spectacular, particularly of the southern peaks of the Swan Crest to the east. Also, some of the peaks of the southeastern portion of the Mission Mountain Wilderness are visible to the northwest.

GETTING THERE

From the intersection of Hwy 35 and Hwy 83, just southeast of Kalispell, drive south on Hwy 83 for 76 miles to Seeley Lake. Drive through Seeley Lake for 1.4 miles. Turn right on Riverview Road and drive west for .7 miles until coming to a fork. Go straight at the fork and continue for another .92 miles until coming to another intersection. If driving to the top, make a right here, and then another right on FS Road #696.

ROUTE INFORMATION

We parked at the next to last intersection. After making the right we hiked for .34 miles until reaching the intersection with FS Road #696. Turning right here, we hiked up the road for an additional 1.29 miles until reaching a closed gate, gaining 604'. Here, there is a trail to the lookout, off to the right. We took the trail, which is a nice break from the hard, rocky road. This added .21 miles and 85' of gain, and some nice views to the west.

PLACID LAKE TO SOUTH

MISSIONS TO NW

SWAN RANGE

SWAN RANGE

EDDY MOUNTAIN

LOLO NATIONAL FOREST

COEUR D'ALENE MOUNTAINS

ELEVATION: 6957' ELEVATION GAIN: 798'
ROUTE DESCRIPTION: ROAD DIFFICULTY: EASY
ROUND TRIP MILEAGE: 3.6 SOLITUDE SCORE: 30

OVERVIEW

This site was first developed in 1931 with an L-4 cab. The current lookout, an R-6 flat cab atop a 10' concrete base, was built in 1982.

Magnificent views await in all four directions! East, the Clark Fork River Valley, south, Cherry Peak, to the west, more of the Coeur D'Alene Mountains, and north, peaks of the Cabinet Mountains Wilderness. North, across the river, Priscilla Peak and the Big Hole Lookout are visible as well.

GETTING THERE

From Plains, drive west on Hwy 200 for 27.6 miles, through Thompson Falls, to Prospect Creek Road. Turn left and drive for 1.48 miles. Turn left on Cherry Creek Road and drive for 5.26 miles until the pavement ends and then turn right on Eddy Peak Road. Drive up Eddy Peak Road for 2.47 miles until the road forks. FS Road #7600 is the upper road to the left and is the correct road. We drove up this narrow, winding, rocky road for 7.24 miles until finding a large pull-out near the top.

ROUTE INFORMATION

We hiked up the road for .94 miles, gaining 389', to a closed gate. Continuing up the road to where it ended was an additional .72 miles, gaining another 304'. The trail up to the lookout was .14 miles, gaining another 105'.

EAST--
CLARK
FORK

NORTH

GARVER MOUNTAIN

KOOTENAI NATIONAL FOREST

PURCELL MOUNTAINS

ELEVATION: 5874' ELEVATION GAIN: 1797'
ROUTE DESCRIPTION: TRAIL DIFFICULTY: MODERATE
ROUND TRIP MILEAGE: 7.62 SOLITUDE SCORE: 30

OVERVIEW

First developed in 1929, with the log cabin currently on the summit. In 1932, a 48' pole tower with a 6x6 cab was built. The current 30' treated timber tower with it's R-6 flat cab was built in 1963.

A fantastic rocky summit area with killer views in every direction! Robinson Mountain to the east, to the southeast is Mount Henry, further south, the Purcells stretch out before you with the Cabinets in the far distance. Westward is the Northwest Peak Scenic Area and to the north are the Canadian Rockies!

GETTING THERE

From Troy, drive 10.2 miles west on Hwy 2. Turn right on Yaak River Road (#508). Drive north on #508 for 26.7 miles until reaching Pete Creek Road (#338). #338 angles in from the left and is hard to see, but is just after Pete Creek CG. Turn left and drive 10.2 miles to the trail head for Trail #8.

ZOOM OF NORTHWEST PEAK

ROUTE INFORMATION

Plunge into the forest on Trail #8 as it quickly begins steeply switchbacking up through trees and several rocky meadows. The trail is well cairned through here. Just short of 1.5 miles and 1000' feet of gain, the first eye-popping views are earned to the south and westward of Davis Mountain and Northwest Peak. Here, the trail makes a hard left (east) and traverses below the ridge top, losing about 100' of gain and then regaining it. At 3.12 miles there is a junction, take the right and head upward. Gain about 536' in .7 miles. This section of trail is rocky and full of roots. Just below the summit, there is another junction, head right again and shortly the summit is reached.

SOUTH

NORTHWEST PEAK SCENIC AREA

ZOOM OF MOUNT
BALDY (BUCKHORN)

WEST

57

GEM PEAK
KANIKSU NATIONAL FOREST
BITTERROOT RANGE

ELEVATION: 6092' ELEVATION GAIN: 973'
ROUTE DESCRIPTION: ROAD DIFFICULTY: EASY
ROUND TRIP MILEAGE: 4.94 SOLITUDE SCORE: 20

OVERVIEW

This site was developed in 1939 with a 20' pole tower with an L-4 cab. Prior to that, there was a 15' pole platform tower with no living quarters. The current 30' treated timber tower with it's R-6 flat cab was built in 1964.

Views from here are quite impressive. The Cabinet Mountains Wilderness to the northeast are book-ended to the northwest by the rugged peaks of the Scotchman area in Montana and Idaho. Just to the southwest, and much closer, are the peaks along the Idaho border, Eighty Peak, Idaho Point, Bottle Point and Ulm Peak. Great hiking if you're renting the lookout or just day hiking in the area!

GETTING THERE

From Plains, drive west on Hwy 200 for approximately 45.8 miles to Fir Street. Turn left, drive for 1.11 miles, then veer left onto Pine Street. Stay on Pine, which eventually becomes Marten Creek Road, for 6.38 miles, until reaching Minton Peak Road (#322). Bear right here and drive for 9.64 miles (bear left after crossing the bridge) to FS Road #2213. Turn right and drive up the mountain 5.57 miles. We parked by the warming hut.

ROUTE INFORMATION

There is an intersection of roads at the warming hut. We chose to hike from here, instead of driving to the top. Take the first road on the right and hike up the road for 2.47 miles, gaining 973' of elevation. We encountered gate posts at 1.95 miles but there was no gate on them.

CABINET MOUNTAINS

IDAHO BORDER PEAKS

ZOOM OF 80 PEAK

ZOOM OF BOTTLE POINT

MOUNT HENRY
KOOTENAI NATIONAL FOREST
PURCELL MOUNTAINS

ELEVATION: 7243' ELEVATION GAIN: 1879'
ROUTE DESCRIPTION: TRAIL DIFFICULTY: MODERATE
ROUND TRIP MILEAGE: 8.48 SOLITUDE SCORE: 10

OVERVIEW

This site was first developed in 1910 with a camp lookout. In 1925, a stone and frame cupola cabin was built. The current 10' pole tower with it's L-4 cab was built in 1942.

Views are expansive! North into Canada, south into the Purcells, west, all the way to Northwest Peak at the Idaho border, and east, on a clear day, the Salish Mountains, the Whitefish Range, and Glacier National Park.

GETTING THERE

From Eureka, drive west on Tobacco Road for .7 miles. Turn right on Othorp Lake Road (#854). Drive across the Salish Mountains for 9.18 miles to MT Hwy 37. Turn left, drive south for 5.05 miles to the Lake Koocanusa Bridge. Turn right onto the bridge. Turn right at the end of the bridge and drive up #92 for 4.12 miles. Take the left fork (#92) and drive 21.08 miles to Solo Joe Road (#6035). Turn left and drive for 2.9 miles. Turn left on #6034 and drive for 4.3 miles until reaching the trail head.

MOUNT HENRY

ROUTE INFORMATION

Hike up Trail #17 for 1.78 miles. Look to the right from here and find a short side trail to Mount Henry Lake. Views are spell binding of the lake set against the steep talus slopes of Mount Henry. Go back and continue hiking up Trail #17. At 3.15 miles, Trail #91 intersects from the south. After hiking for approximately another .5 miles the trail makes a hard right and begins a steep ascent. At 4.02 miles, Trail #9 intersects from the west. The summit heaps it's visual rewards upon the hiker at 4.24 miles....enjoy!

ROBINSON MOUNTAIN

VIEW NORTH

MOUNT HENRY LAKE

KEELER MOUNTAIN
KOOTENAI NATIONAL FOREST
CABINET MOUNTAINS

ELEVATION: 4943' ELEVATION GAIN: 980'
ROUTE DESCRIPTION: ROAD DIFFICULTY: EASY
ROUND TRIP MILEAGE: 7.76 SOLITUDE SCORE: 10

OVERVIEW

This site was first developed in 1924 with a 50' platform tower and a log cabin. In 1934, a 50' pole tower with an L-4 cab was built. The current 53' treated timber tower with an R-6 flat cab was built in 1963.

Tremendous views await in all directions! The higher peaks of the Cabinet Mountains Wilderness fill the eastern horizon from north to south. Interesting perspectives of the two highest peaks in the Cabinets, A and Snowshoe Peaks. To the southwest, the exceptionally rugged peaks of the Scotchman area along the Montana-Idaho border beckon to the adventurous hiker!

GETTING THERE

From Libby, drive west on Hwy 2 for 13.08 miles to MT Hwy 56. Turn left and drive for 5.37 miles to Chase Cut-Off. Turn right and drive for 1.97 miles to Lake Creek Road. Turn left and drive 3.89 miles to unmarked FS Road #473-A. Turn right and drive .24 miles to FS Road #4610. Turn left and drive up the mountain. We drove 4 miles, parking at the switchback.

ZOOM OF UNNAMED PEAK
TO SOUTHWEST

ROUTE INFORMATION

Here, FS Road #4610 magically becomes FS Road #4602. Hike up the road and encounter a locked gate at .78 miles. Continue up the road, hiking up the western flank, around the north end, and eastern flank of the mountain, before curling back around to the top for 3.88 miles one way, gaining 980'. This is a low elevation peak, which could be done early in the season, but FS Road #4610 is not opened until July 10th.

SOUTHEAST

A AND SNOWSHOE PEAKS

DRIFT PEAK

ZOOM OF SNOWSHOE PEAK

MINTON PEAK
KANIKSU NATIONAL FOREST
BITTERROOT RANGE

ELEVATION: 5351' ELEVATION GAIN: 1150'
ROUTE DESCRIPTION: ROAD DIFFICULTY: EASY
ROUND TRIP MILEAGE: 7.18 SOLITUDE SCORE: 30

OVERVIEW

This site was first developed in 1932 with a 10' pole tower with an L-4 cab. This was replaced in the 1950's with a 10' treated timber tower with L-4 cab. The current structure, a replica L-4 cab, was built in 2011.

Views to the north and east of the higher peaks of the Cabinet Mountains Wilderness and other Cabinet peaks are tremendous!

GETTING THERE

The directions are the same as Gem Peak (page 59), until reaching Minton Peak Road (#322). Instead of continuing past this road, turn left and head up the mountain. We drove up for 5.4 miles and parked just past where FS Road #2219 intersects #322.

ROUTE INFORMATION

From there it is an easy road hike for 2.93 miles, gaining 855', reaching the intersection of FS Road #322-A on the right. Hang a right and continue hiking for an additional .66 miles, gaining another 295', until reaching the lookout. We encountered no gates on this hike.

SOUTH

EAST

NORTH

ZOOM OF ROCK AND ELEPHANT PEAKS

MORRELL MOUNTAIN

LOLO NATIONAL FOREST
SWAN RANGE

ELEVATION: 7796' ELEVATION GAIN: 134'
ROUTE DESCRIPTION: ROAD DIFFICULTY: EASY
ROUND TRIP MILEAGE: .8 SOLITUDE SCORE: 20

OVERVIEW

This site was first established in 1921 with a log cupola cabin. The present 10' concrete base with an R-6 flat cab was built in 1962. This is an active lookout that is staffed during fire season.

Expansive and breathtaking vistas surround you! The Swan Crest to the north, the Mission Mountains to the northwest, the Scapegoat Wilderness to the east, the Rattlesnake Wilderness to the southwest, and the Garnet range to the south. A veritable smorgasbord for the eyes!

GETTING THERE

These directions are the same as Double Arrow (page 47). Upon entering Seeley Lake, turn left on Morrell Creek Road and drive for 7.84 miles heading toward Cottonwood Lakes. Turn left on FS Road #4365 and drive up the mountain for 8.46 miles. We parked at the last switchback before the closed gate, making for a very short hike.

MORRELL MOUNTAIN AND LOOKOUT FROM DOUBLE ARROW

ROUTE INFORMATION

Just walk up the road for less than half a mile and enjoy the scenery! Strongly encouraged is the hike over to the actual summit of Morrell, which is less than a mile away up the north ridge and adds only about 600' of gain. If parked at the last switchback, this additional hike is easily achievable and puts one on a summit over 8000' with little effort. If parked lower, use common sense on whether to take on the additional effort.

ZOOM OF
McDONALD
PEAK

MISSION MOUNTAINS

SOUTHEAST

NORTH-MORRELL SUMMIT

SEPTEMBER
2015

NORTHWEST PEAK
KOOTENAI NATIONAL FOREST
PURCELL MOUNTAINS

ELEVATION: 7705' ELEVATION GAIN: 1574'
ROUTE DESCRIPTION: TRAIL DIFFICULTY: MODERATE
ROUND TRIP MILEAGE: 5.38 SOLITUDE SCORE: 20

OVERVIEW

The area was first developed with a camp in 1921. The present building, a gabled L-4 cab prototype, was built in 1929.

At the summit a huge cairn awaits, as well as, mind blowing views in all four directions! Canada to the north, Idaho to the west, Mount Henry and Robinson Mountain to the east, and Davis Mountain and the rest of the Northwest Peak Scenic Area to the south...along with Mount Baldy!

GETTING THERE

These directions are the same as Garver Mountain (page 55). Except, continue driving past the trail head for Garver an additional 18.6 miles to the trail head for Trail #169.

NORTHWEST PEAK FROM THE TRAIL TO GARVER

ROUTE INFORMATION

Hike up Trail #169 as it approaches the summit of Northwest Peak via an eastern ridge. Many large rocks are embedded in the trail, watch your step! After hiking for 2.26 miles and gaining 1215', the base of the vast eastern talus field is reached. Continue up through the talus for .43 miles, gaining 359'. The talus is very stable as decades of hikers have worn a trail into it.

DAVIS MOUNTAIN

NORTHWEST

SOUTHEAST

EAST

PATRICKS KNOB
LOLO NATIONAL FOREST
COEUR D'ALENE MOUNTAINS

ELEVATION: 6836' ELEVATION GAIN: 1025'
ROUTE DESCRIPTION: ROAD DIFFICULTY: EASY
ROUND TRIP MILEAGE: 6.28 SOLITUDE SCORE: 30

OVERVIEW

This site was first developed in 1934 with a 20' pole tower with an L-4 cab. Destroyed in 1968 and replaced with a cupola trailer. The current 10' concrete base with it's R-6 flat cab was built in 1976.

Jaw-dropping vistas reward you at the summit! Baldy Mountain, north of Plains is quite impressive, westward, more of the Coeur D'Alenes and the Bitterroots, and far to the east, the mighty Missions. Northwest, the Cabinets are visible, all the while the Clark Fork River paints a turquoise ribbon along the valley floor.

GETTING THERE

In the town of Plains, turn onto Willis St. Drive .26 miles, veer right onto 5th Ave South and cross the Clark Fork River. After driving .77 miles turn left onto River Road. Drive approximately .1 miles and River Road makes a hard right and becomes Combest Creek Road (#508). This is the road to the top. At approximately 11.1 miles there is an intersection of FS Roads along the ridge. Turn left onto FS Road #7592. We drove another 2.5 miles to the first big switchback and parked. Total mileage from the intersection of Hwy 28 and Hwy 200 is 13.6 miles.

ROUTE INFORMATION

From the switchback, hike up the road for 3.14 miles, gaining 1025', to the lookout, atop it's rocky perch, bypassing the massive electronic site enroute. We saw no gates to bar vehicle progress, so it is possible to drive all the way.

BALDY MOUNTAIN

WEST

EAST

SOUTH

85

PISTOL CREEK
CSKT (FLATHEAD) RESERVATION
MISSION MOUNTAINS

ELEVATION: 6126' ELEVATION GAIN: 1000'
ROUTE DESCRIPTION: ROAD DIFFICULTY: EASY
ROUND TRIP MILEAGE: 8.72 SOLITUDE SCORE: 30

OVERVIEW

This 53' treated timber tower with R-6 flat cab was built in 1970. This lookout is staffed during fire season.

Tremendous, sweeping vistas in every direction! McLeod Peak to the south in the Rattlesnake beckons! Views to the west across the Jocko Valley are superb! But the views to the northeast of the Mission Mountains Wilderness are beyond compare!

GETTING THERE

From Kalispell, we drove down MT Hwy 35 for 49.5 miles to the intersection with Hwy 93 in Polson. Continue south on Hwy 93 for approximately 42.43 miles, turning left on Jocko Road, just south of Arlee. After .13 miles, turn right at the stop sign to stay on Jocko Road. Drive for 2.94 miles, then bear left onto Jocko Canyon Road, where the pavement ends. Drive for 1.51 miles and then turn left to go up the mountain. This is unmarked (June 2016), but just past a cattle guard. We drove up for 4.66 miles, parking at a sharp switchback, encountering an "open gate" at the first mile.

ROUTE INFORMATION

Hike up the road for .97 miles to a fork. Take the left fork and continue up the road. At 2.65 miles, encounter another fork. Take the right fork here, confirmed by a sign on a tree, which is the first confirmation of the correct road. At 3.25 miles, another "open gate" encountered. Continue upward until reaching the lookout tower at 4.36 miles, gaining 1000'.

WEST

ZOOM OF McLEOD PEAK
RATTLESNAKE WILDERNESS

WEST AND EAST ST. MARY PEAK

ZOOM OF GRAY WOLF PEAK

89

PRISCILLA PEAK
LOLO NATIONAL FOREST
CABINET MOUNTAINS

ELEVATION: 7005' ELEVATION GAIN: 4223'
ROUTE DESCRIPTION: TRAIL DIFFICULTY: DIFFICULT
ROUND TRIP MILEAGE: 11.12 SOLITUDE SCORE: 30

OVERVIEW

This site was first developed in 1929, with the cupola cabin that is still standing.

Views from this remote peak are outstanding! Sundance Ridge undulates away to the north, beckoning hikers to Mount Headley. Cube Iron Mountain to the west is also a worthy endeavor. Of course, from this neck of the woods, Baldy Mountain is always a prominent peak!

GETTING THERE

From Plains, drive west on Hwy 200 for 20.65 miles. Turn right onto Thompson River Road (#556). Drive for 9.86 miles to the trail head on the left side of the road. #556 is paved for the first 4.2 miles. Lots of parking available, but more than likely, having to share is a non-issue.

ZOOM OF PRISCILLA PEAK FROM CUBE IRON

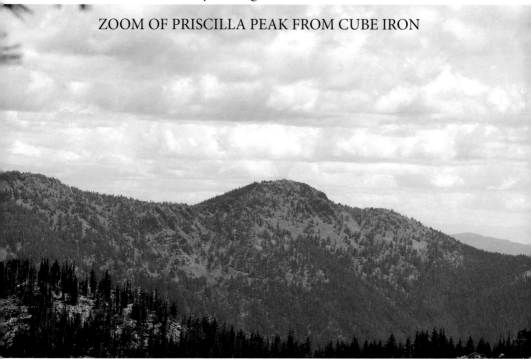

ROUTE INFORMATION

Probably, the favorite and the most difficult in the book. This one has to be earned with some sweat equity! This peak has a remote feel about it that many of the others lack.

Basically, grind your way up the trail for 5.56 miles to the summit. One minor issue, at one point the trail enters some old logging scar/slash, and is easy to lose here, we did lose it. We continued up through the slash, knowing the trail was to the left, and found it again when we needed to.

91

NORTH-SUNDANCE RIDGE

CLIFFS NEAR MT. HEADLEY

SOUTHEAST

WEST-CUBE IRON MOUNTAIN

RICHARDS PEAK

LOLO NATIONAL FOREST
CABINET MOUNTAINS

ELEVATION: 5771' ELEVATION GAIN: 1881'
ROUTE DESCRIPTION: ROAD DIFFICULTY: MODERATE
ROUND TRIP MILEAGE: 9.62 SOLITUDE SCORE: 30

OVERVIEW

This site was first established in 1925 with a cupola cabin. The current 10' concrete base with the R-6 flat cab was built in 1960.

Views from this summit are stupendous! To the northwest, the high peaks of the Cabinet Mountains Wilderness can be seen. To the west and south more of the wild and rugged lower Cabinet peaks similar to Richards. North and northeast, more of the Cabinets and the Salish Mountains. Best views are to the southeast into the Thompson Peak area, along with Cook Mountain. Farther to the southeast, the ever present Baldy Mountain, once again, makes for an inviting future destination!

GETTING THERE

From Kalispell, drive west on Hwy 2 for 38.8 miles. Turn left on the Thompson River Road (#56). Drive for 14.69 miles until reaching FS Road #1045. Turn right and drive for 3.89 miles. At this point, there is a sign for FS Road #7573 and a right turn. DO NOT TURN RIGHT! Continue straight ahead as #1045 becomes #7573 and this is the way to the lookout. We drove up #7573 for .84 miles and parked in a large pullout.

OPEN DOOR
LOO VIEW

ROUTE INFORMATION

From here, this is just a straightforward road hike to the top for almost 5 miles one way, gaining 1881'. We did encounter a gate after hiking 4.2 miles. This is an excellent spring conditioning hike!

ZOOM OF SNOWSHOE AND A PEAKS

NORTHWEST

EAST-THE THOMPSON PEAK AREA

BALDY MOUNTAIN

ROBINSON MOUNTAIN
KOOTENAI NATIONAL FOREST
PURCELL MOUNTAINS

ELEVATION: 7539' ELEVATION GAIN: 2152'
ROUTE DESCRIPTION: ROAD, TRAIL DIFFICULTY: MODERATE
ROUND TRIP MILEAGE: 10.36 SOLITUDE SCORE: 20

OVERVIEW

First established with a camp in 1921. The shake cupola cabin, still standing, was built in 1929.

Views are quite rewarding! North into Canada, east across Lake Koocanusa are the Salish Mountains, and further east is the Whitefish Range. To the southwest, Mount Henry looks quite impressive! South and west are more of the Purcell Mountains.

GETTING THERE

The directions for reaching Robinson are the same as Mount Henry (see page 63), until reaching the fork in #92. To reach Robinson, take the right fork (#474) and drive for 2.12 miles and #474 becomes #470. Continue on #470 for an additional 8.18 miles, then turn right onto FS Road #7205. Continue up #7205 for 1.6 miles until reaching "gated" #999 on the left.

ZOOM FROM THE NOTCH

ROUTE INFORMATION

Hike up closed FS Road #999 for 1.94 miles, gaining 369', until reaching the third (of three trail heads) for Trail #59. Hike up Trail #59 for 1.35 miles, gaining 468', until reaching the junction with Trail #58 coming in from the north. Turn left here and head up .69 miles and 633' to a notch in the ridge. The upper portion of this trail is steep and loose. From the notch, the trail traverses the ridge to the southeast corner of the summit block and then switchbacks up the south face for 1.2 miles and 682'.

SOUTHWEST

SOUTH

ZOOM OF MOUNT HENRY

MAY 2015

SEX PEAK
KANIKSU NATIONAL FOREST
BITTERROOT RANGE

ELEVATION: 5772' ELEVATION GAIN: 1141'
ROUTE DESCRIPTION: ROAD DIFFICULTY: EASY
ROUND TRIP MILEAGE: 8.64 SOLITUDE SCORE: 20

OVERVIEW

First established with an L-4 cab in 1930. The present L-4 cab was built in 1948.

Stunning scenery all around along with a fluttering American flag paint an almost surreal scene at this summit! Views to the east across the Clark Fork River, of the Cabinets and some to the north, of the higher peaks of the Cabinet Mountains Wilderness. To the south, Clear Peak is impressive, and to the west, Black Peak, on the Idaho border, cuts a dominating figure above surrounding peaks.

GETTING THERE

From Plains, drive west on Hwy 200 for 36.6 miles to Big Beaver Creek Road. Turn left and drive for 10.6 miles until reaching FS Road #2222. Turn right and head up the mountain. We drove up 4.6 miles and parked.

ROUTE INFORMATION

After hiking up the road for 4.32 miles and gaining 1141' in elevation the summit is reached. Views will greet you on the road, well before the summit, particularly to the south and west. Another great spring conditioning hike!

103

BLACK PEAK ON IDAHO BORDER

ZOOM OF
CARNEY PEAK
AND LOST BUCK
PASS

ZOOM OF CLEAR PEAK

SONYOK MOUNTAIN
CSKT (FLATHEAD) RESERVATION
SALISH MOUNTAINS

ELEVATION: 5657' ELEVATION GAIN: 1794'
ROUTE DESCRIPTION: ROAD DIFFICULTY: MODERATE
ROUND TRIP MILEAGE: 8.96 SOLITUDE SCORE: 30

OVERVIEW

This site was first developed in 1935 with a cabin. Replaced in the 1970's with the current 20' treated timber tower with flat cab. This is known as the Ferry Basin Lookout.

Mere words can't do justice to what will be seen here. The Reservation is shockingly beautiful, the Mission Valley and the Mission Range to the east, the Reservation Divide peaks to the south, the Flathead River...WOW!!

GETTING THERE

From Kalispell, drive south on Hwy 93 for 35.2 miles to Hwy 28 at Elmo. Turn right and drive for 30.38 miles to Hwy 382, 2.5 miles south of Hot Springs. Turn left and drive for 15.47 miles to Race Horse Gulch Road, the last road on the left before the bridge crossing the Flathead River. Turn left. We drove up this road for 7.93 miles to a fork and parked. This road is not good, don't be fooled by the beginning, good tires definitely needed!

ROUTE INFORMATION

From here, hike up the right fork for 2.42 miles, gaining 945'. Round the corner and head east, losing 196' of elevation. Continue hiking east from the lowest point and regain the lost elevation and more. There was a closed gate at 4.2 miles. Continue past the gate for an additional .24 miles while rounding the summit outcrops only to be greeted by several flights of stairs! Once reaching the base of the lookout, an additional 653' has been gained, and the 196' lost on the way up must be regained on the way back.

MISSION VALLEY

ZOOM OF McDONALD PEAK

NATIONAL BISON RANGE

NORTH

STAR PEAK
KOOTENAI NATIONAL FOREST
CABINET MOUNTAINS

ELEVATION: 6167' ELEVATION GAIN: 3916'
ROUTE DESCRIPTION: ROAD, TRAIL DIFFICULTY: DIFFICULT
ROUND TRIP MILEAGE: 11.58 SOLITUDE SCORE: 20

OVERVIEW

First developed in 1907 with a camp. The stone cabin below the summit was built in 1910. In 1930, the first L-4 cab was built on the summit. The current L-4 cab was constructed in 1952.

Mind blowing vistas greet the hardy hiker at the summit! Billiard Table Mountain to the north looks bizarre with it's tilted summit. To the northeast, the Cabinet Mountains Wilderness stretches for miles. To the southeast, the Clark Fork River becomes the Cabinet Gorge Reservoir. Looking west and south, the Bitterroots rise up along the Idaho-Montana border.

GETTING THERE

From Plains, drive west on Hwy 200 for 66.2 miles to Hwy 56. Continue past Hwy 56 an additional 4.38 miles to a large pullout on the left. Park here and walk back east along Hwy 200 a few yards and cross it where FS Road #2721 is visible. This is the beginning of the arduous hike to the top.

ROUTE INFORMATION

Hike up the steep, rocky road for 2.58 miles gaining approximately 2000', to where the actual Trail #998 begins. The trail is actually less steep than the road! At 3.13 miles there is an intersecting trail coming in from the left, make sure you take the correct one on the way back down. Reach the summit (formerly Squaw Peak) and it's talus piles at approximately 5.79 miles. Prepare to be mesmerized by what you are about to witness!

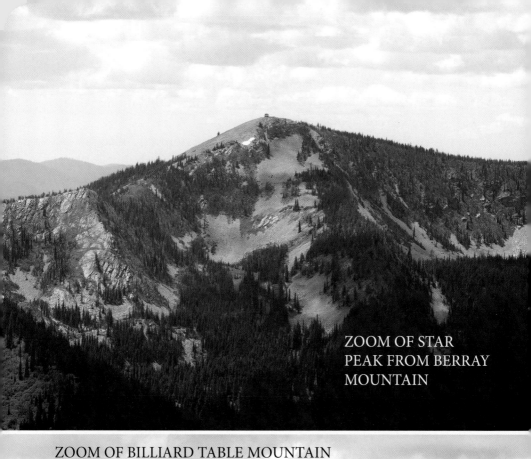

ZOOM OF STAR
PEAK FROM BERRAY
MOUNTAIN

ZOOM OF BILLIARD TABLE MOUNTAIN

SOUTHEAST

NORTHEAST

113

STARK MOUNTAIN
LOLO NATIONAL FOREST
NINEMILE DIVIDE

ELEVATION: 7349' ELEVATION GAIN: 2124'
ROUTE DESCRIPTION: ROAD DIFFICULTY: MODERATE
ROUND TRIP MILEAGE: 9.90 SOLITUDE SCORE: 20

OVERVIEW

This site was first developed in 1934 with a 30' pole tower with an L-4 cab. The current 20' treated timber tower with an R-6 flat cab was built in 1964. It may be staffed during fire season.

Views are incredible in all four directions! Up and down the Ninemile Valley, across to the peaks of the Reservation Divide, and behind them the higher peaks of the Missions. To the south, the Bitterroots are calling!

GETTING THERE

From St. Regis, drive east on Interstate 90 for approximately 27.3 miles to the Tarkio exit #61. Turn left off the ramp, continue past Frontage Road, then bear left on Nemote Creek Road for 1.32 miles. Turn right at the sign for the lookout, onto Nemote Creek Road (#454). Stay on this road, pavement ends at 1.15 miles, stay left at 3.3 miles, stay left at 4.66 miles, bear right at 5.66 miles, and at 6.84 miles the first switchback up the mountain is encountered. We drove up the mountain for 3.99 miles and parked at a switchback.

ROUTE INFORMATION

Hike up the road for 4.95 miles to the summit and the lookout, gaining 2124' in elevation from where we started. There was a closed gate at 2.12 miles. At 3.62 miles, Trail #58 intersects the road from the left. We chose to hike the road due to time constraints. There is at least one other trail that accesses the mountain from the Ninemile Valley side.

ZOOM OF THREE LAKES PEAK

ZOOM OF BLACKROCK PEAK

NINEMILE VALLEY

ZOOM OF CH-PAA-QN PEAK

THOMPSON PEAK
LOLO NATIONAL FOREST
BITTERROOT RANGE

ELEVATION: 4560' ELEVATION GAIN: 747'
ROUTE DESCRIPTION: ROAD DIFFICULTY: EASY
ROUND TRIP MILEAGE: 5.32 SOLITUDE SCORE: 30

OVERVIEW

This site was first developed in 1920 with a tree platform tower. A 30' pole tower with an L-4 cab replaced it in 1934. That was replaced by the current 20' concrete base with flat cab in 1984.

Unable to get into the tower, the best views from the summit around the base of the tower are to the south and southwest into the Bitterroots.

GETTING THERE

From St. Regis, drive east on Interstate 90 for approximately 13.3 miles... departing 90 at Superior exit #47. Turn right off the ramp and then a quick left onto Diamond Match Road. Drive for 1.34 miles to Cedar Creek Road (#320). Turn right and drive for 2.55 miles to FS Road #7863. Turn right, and bear left (staying on #7863) at the intersecting FS Roads. We drove up the mountain for 3.73 miles until reaching a large pullout on the left.

ROUTE INFORMATION

Hike up the road and encounter a closed gate after 1.26 miles. Continue hiking for another 1.4 miles to the summit and the lookout. This is a good early season conditioning hike, but unless you're renting the lookout, views here will not compare to others in the book.

ZOOM TO SOUTHWEST

UP UP MOUNTAIN
LOLO NATIONAL FOREST
BITTERROOT RANGE

ELEVATION: 5969' ELEVATION GAIN: 738'
ROUTE DESCRIPTION: ROAD DIFFICULTY: EASY
ROUND TRIP MILEAGE: 6.76 SOLITUDE SCORE: 20

OVERVIEW

This site was first developed in 1934 with an L-4 cab on a 20' pole tower. The current 41' treated timber tower with it's R-6 flat cab was built in 1966.

Gold, Eagle and Ward Peaks are visible to the south, more of the Bitterroots to the west, and to the north, Cherry and Penrose Peaks. Up close and to the east is Moon Peak.

GETTING THERE

From St. Regis, drive west on Interstate 90 to Exit 22. Get off of I-90 here and then get back on eastbound I-90, and proceed east to Exit 26. Exit here and drive up Ward Creek Road (#889) for 3.17 miles. Turn right on FS Road #3816 and head up the mountain. This is a long and tedious drive. At approximately 10.07 miles we arrived at an intersection. Bear left here. We drove for another 1.08 miles and parked at an open gate (June 2016).

ROUTE INFORMATION

Hike up the road from here. Immediately begin losing elevation, in fact, for the first 1.7 miles, there is a gradual loss of about 240'. From the low point, continue up the road for another 1.68 miles, gaining 498'.... remembering that the 240' lost must be regained on the way back out.

SOUTH

NORTH

WEBB MOUNTAIN
KOOTENAI NATIONAL FOREST
PURCELL MOUNTAINS

ELEVATION: 5988' ELEVATION GAIN: 3341'
ROUTE DESCRIPTION: TRAIL DIFFICULTY: DIFFICULT
ROUND TRIP MILEAGE: 10.0 SOLITUDE SCORE: 20

OVERVIEW

First developed in 1930 with a "redi-cut" cab. The current 10' concrete base with an R-6 flat cab replaced the prior structure in 1959.

Views to the west, north and south of the Purcell Mountains. To the east, over Lake Koocanusa, lie the Salish Mountains, and further east the Whitefish Range.

GETTING THERE

From Eureka, the directions are the same as for Robinson Mountain (see page 99), until coming to the west end of the Lake Koocanusa Bridge. Turn left (south) onto #228 and drive south for 1.32 miles. When we hiked this (2012) the trail head was unmarked from the north and we passed it up. A tip, from the north, the trail head is the first pullout on the right after Boulder Creek.

ROUTE INFORMATION

Hike up Trail #435 for 4.93 miles until reaching the road just below the lookout, gaining 3288'. In 2012, this trail needed lots of work. In many places it was little more than rock-filled, watery ditch. There are lots of switchbacks which help ease the elevation gain to some degree.

NORTH

EAST-BEARTRAP MOUNTAIN

WEST

SOUTH

YAAK MOUNTAIN
KOOTENAI NATIONAL FOREST
PURCELL MOUNTAINS

ELEVATION: 4995' ELEVATION GAIN: 2030'
ROUTE DESCRIPTION: ROAD DIFFICULTY: MODERATE
ROUND TRIP MILEAGE: 11.82 SOLITUDE SCORE: 30

OVERVIEW

This site was first developed in 1914 as a camp. In 1915, a 45' pole platform came next. In 1919, a cupola cabin was built. In the 1930's, a 50' pole tower with L-6 cab with a log cabin was built. The current 41' treated timber tower with R-6 flat cab was constructed in 1958.

Views to the southeast of the Cabinet Mountains Wilderness are tremendous! Purcells to the north and east, and Idaho to the west.

GETTING THERE

From Troy, drive west on Hwy 2 for 3.76 miles to the East Side Road. Turn right and drive for 1.71 miles to Lake Kilbrennan Road. Turn right and drive for 2.39 miles to the pullout for FS Road #4407 on the left.

YAAK MOUNTAIN FROM HWY 2

ROUTE INFORMATION

FS Road #4407 is gated and locked. Head up the road, after the first curve, the road heads north. At 3.25 miles the road switchbacks to the south and at 4.2 miles the lookout can be seen in the distance. After 5.91 miles and gaining 2030', the summit and the lookout are reached.

ZOOM OF "A" PEAK

NORTH

ZOOM OF PULPIT MOUNTAIN

ZIEGLER MOUNTAIN
KOOTENAI NATIONAL FOREST
PURCELL MOUNTAINS

ELEVATION: 5394' ELEVATION GAIN: 1374'
ROUTE DESCRIPTION: ROAD DIFFICULTY: EASY
ROUND TRIP MILEAGE: 9.84 SOLITUDE SCORE: 30

OVERVIEW

This site was first developed with a log cabin and a three-legged platform in 1915. A 30' L-4 pole tower was built in 1933. The current 30' treated timber tower with R-6 flat cab was constructed in 1959.

Outstanding views of the Salish Mountains up and down the east side of Lake Koocanusa from the summit. The high peaks of the Cabinet Mountains Wilderness can be seen to the south and southwest. West and north lie the Purcells.

GETTING THERE

From Kalispell, drive west on Hwy 2 for 51 miles to McKillop Road. Turn right and drive for 7.8 miles, then bear right onto FS Road #763. Drive for 6.01 miles until reaching a stop sign. Turn left and continue on #763 an additional 9.96 miles until reaching the stop sign at Hwy 37. Turn left, cross the bridge for .78 miles, then turn right onto #228. Drive up #228 for 15.77 miles til reaching FS Road #4874. Turn left and drive up #4874 for 7.38 miles til reaching FS Road #4815 angling in on the right and park.

ROUTE INFORMATION

Hike along the road and begin losing elevation immediately. This continues for about 1.5 miles, losing 376'. Gradually this is regained as the hike continues eastward along the road. There are no views until reaching the summit which is done via a series of rocky switchbacks up the road.

SOUTH-LAKE KOOCANUSA

ZOOM OF SNOWSHOE AND "A" PEAKS

IN MEMORIAM

TONY PEAK

MAY 2014

We hiked to the top of Tony Peak in search of the Tony Peak Lookout in May 2014. Upon doing the historical research for the lookout it came to our attention that the lookout had been involved in a fire later in the same year. Forest service personnel for the Libby Ranger District of the Kootenai National Forest confirmed that it had been totally destroyed in the fire. What a shame!

In any event, we still felt it worthwhile to include, as it is still a fantastic hike up the mountain with some really unique views. Breathtaking views of the Cabinet Mountains Wilderness to the west, the Libby Dam to the north, and to the southeast, the Salish Mountains across the Fisher River.

This is not an easy hike and when we did it, involved some minor bushwhacking along with some route finding skills. Without going into specifics about where the trail is lost and regained, suffice it to say, that while most of the mileage and elevation gain is on trail (2.55 miles...1910'), that some is a bushwhack off trail (.87 miles...728'). Much of this is steep, and definitely not recommended as a first or early season hike.....your legs will thank you for waiting until they're less rusty!

The trail head for #582 is located off FS Road #763 on Champion-Haul Road (Google Earth). It is also possible to drive up to the electronic site just below the summit on FS Road #533, also located off of FS Road #763. Google Earth shows the lookout still present on 7-11-14. The 10' pole tower with L-4 cab was built in 1934 and was the only one built there.

LIBBY DAM

SALISH MOUNTAINS

ZOOM OF THE CABINET MOUNTAINS WILDERNESS

MEET THE PHOTOGRAPHER

I count myself fortunate and blessed every day I rise, knowing that this fine lady is my wife and best friend. Even better, we get to spend our life together haunting the woods of Montana. Lynne's fervent love of the outdoors, I believe, is captured in the many images of this book. There is no one that I would rather be out there with than her. Time and again, she has proven to be a reliable and capable partner. In more than one instance, (i.e. grizzlies) where many men would have melted in their tracks or run away crying for their mommies, this woman has stood by my side and had my back.

Lynne has reached the summit of 182 mountains throughout northwest Montana and one in Idaho, as of the writing of this book. Once on the trail, there are few things that would or could stop her from reaching her goal. More than once she has gone out there sick or injured and still managed to obtain the goal of the high point of the mountain. To this point, after hiking over 1500 miles in all of the various mountain ranges in northwest Montana, her favorite is the Whitefish Range, for it's true wilderness feeling.

Two fixed lens cameras are used, a Canon Powershot SX130 IS and a Nikon Coolpix P510. Since they are fixed lens cameras they do not show the true steepness of a slope or mountain.   ----Steve Rains

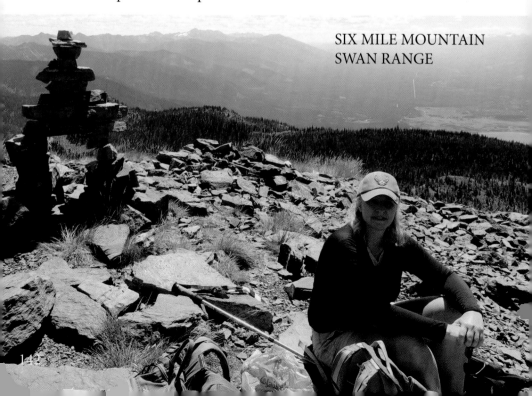

SIX MILE MOUNTAIN
SWAN RANGE

MEET THE AUTHOR

Mountain fever gets in your bones. The author has an acute case of this fever. He has always had an intense love of the outdoors. That love, combined with his affection for writing, has enabled him, along with his lovely photographer, to produce three books on hiking in beautiful northwest Montana.

Every season they hit the various mountain ranges with the best intentions and a rather long list of unachievable goals. During the winter months you might find him poring over his ever growing collection of maps and Google Earth, planning and creating the next season's list of unachievable goals. As of the writing of this book, he has summitted 194 mountains in northwest Montana and one in Idaho, and hiked in the neighborhood of 2000 miles. Not one to necessarily have to climb the tallest or most popular peaks in the area, he would rather search out some remote mountain that most people have never heard of, and, if it is difficult to get to, that much the better.

When not out there trying to get to the top of something, he also enjoys hunting, fishing, and driving really fast!

RED BENCHMARK
WHITEFISH RANGE